AURORA

WHAT HAPPENED TO THE HEART?

DECCA

FABER *ff* MUSIC

WHAT HAPPENED TO THE HEART?

WHAT happened to the heart?

I found myself in a dark place.
I felt alone.
And not like myself.

The more time I spent in there I learned that the dark place
that seemed to go on forever, had walls.
Traces of what used to be windows and doors all around me.

With time I noticed the others.
There were so many people here, that I hadn't even noticed.
We were somehow all here together, yet alone.
What happened to us?
And how did we end up here?

We called out through the cracks in the ceiling but found no compassion in the
eyes of the people looking down at us. We tried to carve open our windows
and got pushed down for trying to stand up for ourselves.

We don't see each other like we should.
And we don't feel each other.
And when we do see each other, something strange lies in the way
of the invisible lines that should tie our hearts together.

And I wondered why is it so hard for us?
To love ourselves. And to love each other.
To connect to the earth around us, and every living thing in it.

We're all just sitting in the dark, thinking we're alone.

But we are not alone.
We never were.
And we never will be.

Who led us here?
And how could we fail each other so deeply?
Our ancestors and our past.
The indigenous voices speaking truths older than time.
Our children, our future.
Ourselves.

It seems we have forgotten the true value we carry within us, the true value
of our time here on earth and how not to waste it away. The true value
of the people and cultures and voices that coexist with us.
It's all so wrapped up in power.

The power of money.
The power of beauty.
The power of lying without ever getting caught.
The power of violence.
The power of fear.

And as I sat there in the dark, I decided to write. I needed to write something good
to myself. And also something good to the people who sat in the dark with me.

And it all began with a very large question.

What happened to the heart?

AURORA
June 2024

WHAT HAPPENED

TO THE

HEART?

Aristotle - the heart creates
the blood?

Platon - the heart circulates
the blood?

Hippocrates - the heart brings
the blood through
the body to the lungs

MENON

the HEART pumps blood
with a rhythm.

the spiritual

Eristratos - the heart is
a pump?

THE UNANGAN ELDERS referred to the heart as a
~~source~~ source of wisdom. And a deeper
portal of profound interconnectedness and awareness
that exists between humans and all living things.

as

the HEART is a muscular organ in most animals.
divided into 4 chambers.
in humans the heart is
approximately the size of
a closed fist between the lungs.
Humans have known abot the heart,

since ancient times.

Allthough its precise function
and anatomy were not clearly
understood. The Heart was believed to be the center

of emotion.
of the soul.
our consiousness
of intention.

UNTIL we decided these
were qualifications of the mind.
Indigenous leaders from around
the world came together in
2020 with the message that
Humans needs to shift from the
mind to the heart. let our heart lead us.

What happened to the heart?

It's the most important, beautiful and
sad question I've ever wondered in my life.

"LISTEN TO YOUR HEART
FOLLOW YOUR PATH

MAY IT BE CLEAR
AND FOR THE GOOD
OF ALL"

Echo Of My Shadow

If I stay here any longer
I will stay here forever
And the echo of my world will fade
Will the edge of my sorrow
Be gone in the morning?
I know

Stay right here
Stay in the light my dear
Until the love you crave
Falls in your arms
I know your mind
Moves like a wave sometimes
If you can't rise for us
Do it for love

If my life is just a moment
And this world is ancient
Then the light through my window will fade
Young mountains, old rivers
I let them become me
Right now

Stay right here
Stay in the light my dear
Until the love you crave
Falls in your arms
I know your mind
Moves like a wave sometimes
If you can't rise for us
Do it for love

If I stay here any longer
I will stay here forever
Till the echo of my shadow is gone
There are heroes within us
There are lovers around us
They will be here forever
I know
I know
I know

Echo of my shadow —

I told my friend Martin
I had a song in my mind
Something that sounded
like the first moment of
sunrise, where its orange light
hits the top of a mountain
and slowly makes her
way down.
Heating up the cold stone.
erasing shadows.
little by little.

this is what I hear
in the depths of my mind
when this happens.
Thank you Bergen, my
Hometown for letting me
see this, every day, if I
want to.

POTENTIAL SONGS:

1. THE ECHO OF MY SHADOW
2. YOUR BLOOD
3.
4. CONFLICT OF THE MIND
5. EARTHLY DELIGHTS
6. MY NAME
7.
8. PULSE
9. DETERIORATION
10. INVISIBLE WOUNDS
11. PIANO SANG
12.
13.

I find myself bothered with the lack of atonomy in my titles. What Am I scared of reaching for?

THE STORY OF "I"
♥ TO FEEL ALLRIGHT
♥ SOULSEARCHER
I CANT UNTIE
THE DARK THAT FOLLOWS
QUIET NOISE
DRAWN TO YOU
HEART
(NO TRUST)
FORGET YOUR BODY

SOME TYPE OF SKIN

Hit me hard where I am soft
Should my heart reveal itself to be more than a muscle?
Or a fist covered in blood?
However much it feels to bleed
It's only temporary

We're good people and we both deserve peace

My god! It's a lot!
(To build some type of skin
I got to build some type of skin)
My god! It's a lot!
(To build some type of skin
I got to build some type of skin)

I guess I should build some type of skin
And let breath be air and love the things I know might disappear
And the last light of the sun
I let it slow me down
I'll crawl where everybody runs

We're good people and we deserve peace
It's difficult it seems

My god! It's a lot!
(To build some type of skin
I got to build some type of skin)
My god! It's a lot!
(To build some type of skin
I got to build some type of skin)
My god!
(To build some type of skin
I got to build some type of skin)
My god! It's a lot!
(To build some type of skin
I got to build some type of skin)

It's a lot, a lot to me

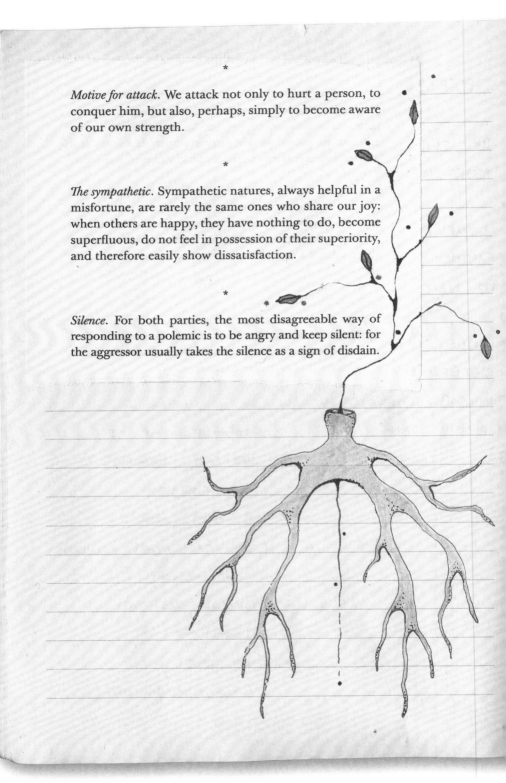

Motive for attack. We attack not only to hurt a person, to conquer him, but also, perhaps, simply to become aware of our own strength.

*

The sympathetic. Sympathetic natures, always helpful in a misfortune, are rarely the same ones who share our joy: when others are happy, they have nothing to do, become superfluous, do not feel in possession of their superiority, and therefore easily show dissatisfaction.

*

Silence. For both parties, the most disagreeable way of responding to a polemic is to be angry and keep silent: for the aggressor usually takes the silence as a sign of disdain.

"Some type of Skin"

Hit me hard when I am soft
Should my heart, reveal ... itself ... to be
More than a Muscle
or a fist covered in blood
However much it feels
to bleed .... its only temporary.

We're good people
and We both deserve
peace.

MY GOD! ITS ALOT!!!

(build some type of skin .. I got to build some type of skin)

(HAHA) I guess I should build some
type of skin ...
Let breath, be air
"We're good people   and love, the things I know
and we deserve peace"   might disappear
And the last light of the sun
I let it slow me down
I'll crawl ...
...Where everybody runs.

Your Blood

Your blood
What matter is it made of?
Do you feel it travel
In and out your heart?
Needles
Stitching up the big holes
You prepared for battle
As you fell apart

Are you dust?
You are dust

Your voice
Drowning in the white noise
Do you hear the echo
Begging you to let go?
This earth
Whoever was it made for?
Just wait until tomorrow
You might not be as cold

When all inside you burns like a star
It's after you burn out that you are
Reborn again, reborn again
And maybe if you called out for help
Then I could help you outrun yourself
Come run again! We'll run again!

But I, I refuse to die
I refuse to die
But I, I refuse to die
I refuse to die

We are dust
We are dust

When all inside you burns like a star
It's after you burn out that you are
Reborn again, reborn again
And maybe if you called out for help
Then I could help you outrun yourself
Come run again! Come run again!

You are dust…

Your blood
What matter is it made of?
Do you feel it travel
In and out your heart?

YOUR BLOOD

your blood
What matter is it made of?
do you feel it travel?
in and out your heart?
Needles... stiching up the big holes
you prepared for battle
as you fell apart...
Are you dust?

"let all inside you
burn like a star
it's after you burn
out, that you are
reborn again

your voice
drowning in the white noise
do you hear the echo?
begging you to let go
this earth
whoever was it made for?
just wait until tomorrow
it might not be a cold

And maybe it you
called out for help
then I could help
you outrun yourself
come run again!!
we'll run again!!

"BUT I, I REFUSE TO DIE"

I REFUSE TO DIE

CHRISTI
TESTA
MENTA

Blood

The fiery soul in its natural primal state – represented in the lower inverted heart – lies "in the Father's quality" in the fire of wrath. Through the sacrament of baptism, however, the name Jesus is revealed in the name Jehovah, and the soul receives the son's fire of love: "The father baptizes with fire, the son with light." His heavenly blood transforms anger into love.

Man must, in his imagination, completely enter into Christ's sacrificial death, "thus there will grow (...) a true Christ, a grape on Christ's vine".

J. Böhme, Theosophische Wercke, Amsterdam, 1682

Opus Magnum: Blood

200PBP-09

The Conflict
Of The Mind

It's a complicated story
That we never talk about
But I see it in the mirrors
In the curtains of our house
I don't want you to be worried
That we're running out of time
It doesn't matter where we're going
We can leave it all behind

Only when I see you cry, I feel conflicted in my mind
It fills my heart up and it breaks me at the very same time
When you open up the gates for me and leave the world behind
We find proof of love is hidden in the conflict of the mind

I remember how I'd find you
Fingers tearing through the ground
Were you digging something up
Or did you bury something down?
In your soul I found a thirst
With only salt inside your cup
In your eyes I saw a longing
While I longed to lift you up?

Only when I see you cry, I feel conflicted in my mind
It fills my heart up and it breaks me at the very same time
When you open up the gates for me and leave the world behind
We find proof of love is hidden in the conflict of the mind

Don't let your spirit die
This is just a conflict of the mind
Is your heart alive?
You'll overcome a conflict of the mind
(Love is not gone, not gone)
(Love is... YOU)

14/2/2023

Only When I see
you cry — I feel conflicted
in my mind

It fills my heart up
and it breaks me at the
very same time

When you open up the
Gates for me
and leave the world behind

Where find proof of love
is Hidden

In the conflict
of the mind

CONFLICT OF THE MIND

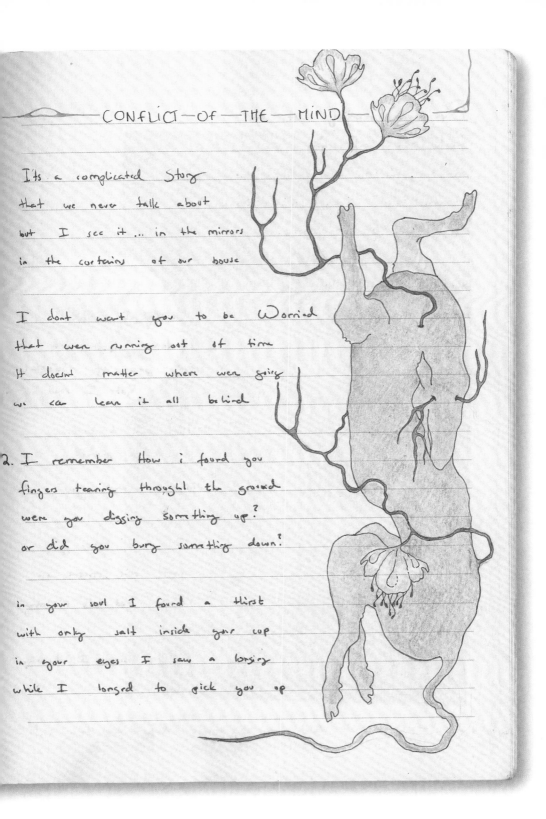

It's a complicated story
that we never talk about
but I see it ... in the mirrors
in the curtains of our house

I don't want you to be worried
that were running out of time
It doesn't matter where were going
we can leave it all behind

2. I remember How i found you
fingers tearing throught the ground
were you digging something up?
or did you bury something down?

in your soul I found a thirst
with only salt inside your cup
in your eyes I saw a longing
while I longed to pick you up

I've been reading alot of
books of alchemy
an the history of occult knowledge
Humans have been so spiritually
hightened for so long.

How on earth did we
forget so much?

Usually I would
condemn ripping out
any page of a book...
But I saw my

"There will a burning
light be poured

into me, and you"

I dont know yet
what this means, or
how i put it in my
album.
I just know I deeply
want to.

This three-legged person . is the best thing I've seen all day

Caution of free spirits. Free-spirited people, living for knowledge alone, will soon find they have achieved their external goal in life, their ultimate position vis à vis society and the state, and gladly be satisfied, for example, with a minor position or a fortune that just meets their needs; for they will set themselves up to live in such a way that a great change in economic conditions, even a revolution in political structures, will not overturn their life with it. They expend as little energy as possible on all these things, so that they can plunge with all their assembled energy, as if taking a deep breath, into the element of knowledge. They can then hope to dive deep, and also get a look at the bottom.

Such a spirit will be happy to take only the corner of an experience; he does not love things in the whole breadth and prolixity of their folds; for he does not want to get wrapped up in them.

He, too, knows the week-days of bondage, dependence, and service. But from time to time he must get a Sunday of freedom, or else he will not endure life.

33

IDEAS

I've spent many hours
    admiring stars ... and ...
I wonder why dreamers
keep dreaming of mars

A world where her life
could've never begun
    Cause they placed her
    a little too far
        from the Sun

Soulsearcher
09/09/2023

So What happened to the heart?

Its hard to look at the world
trying to fix itself while falling apart.

We cannot even fix ourselves.

How is it, with all the spiritual guidiance
and knowledge.
built up through so
many generations
We are still struggling
to truly bring this
World forward.

I refuse to believe
the people on this
earth actually liv
on the same planet.
No connection.
what so ever.
We need an awakening.

Why are we so afraid
to speak up?
this world is out of its
mind.

Whatever draws you to us, you
are always welcome

the wish to draw oneself up with everyone else
(by appreciating, helping, taking pleasure in others'
success).

TO BE ALRIGHT

I know I belong here on earth
But I long to be lifted up
My heart does not rhyme
The rhythm of my mind
What is life worth living
If you can't dance to anything?
Night after night
Oh, I long to be alright

I want to feel it, to feel it
What the people talk about
How do you find it so easy?
And all I can is ask...

But whatever you say it's never right, so I won't do that
(You cannot make me feel a thing)
And wherever I go, I'm always blind, so I lose my track
(You cannot make me feel alright)

How I hunger for touch
How could you say that I love too much?
I don't want to fight
I just want to feel alright
What is life worth living
If you don't bleed for anything?
Night after night
Oh, I long to be alright

I want to feel it, to feel it
What the people talk about
How do you find it so easy?
And all I can is ask...

But whatever you say it's never right, so I won't do that
(You cannot make me feel a thing)
And wherever I go, I'm always blind, so I lose my track
(You cannot make me feel alright)

I love it… I believe I love it
I believe I love it
Nobody can make me feel it so much
I believe I love it
I believe I love it
Nobody can make ME FEEL

I don't want to fight
I just want to feel alright!

What is life worth living
If you don't dance to anything?
Night after night
Oh, I long to feel alright!

27/01/2023

TO FEEL ALLRIGHT

I know I belong here on earth
But I long to be lifted up
My heart does not rhyme
the rhytm of my mind

What is life worth living?
if you don't dance to anything
night after night
Oh I long to feel allright

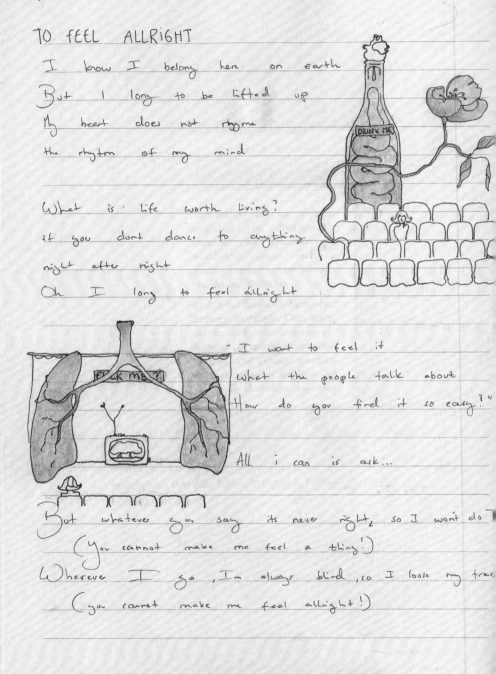

"I want to feel it
what the people talk about
How do you find it so easy?"

All i can is ask...

But whatever you say its never right, so I won't do
(you cannot make me feel a thing!)
Wherever I go, I'm always blind, so I loose my trac
(you cannot make me feel allright!)

How I hunger for touch
How could you say that I love too much?
I dont want to fight.
I just want to feel allright

What is life worth living?
if you dont bleed for anything?
Night after night
OH I LONG TO FEEL ALLRIGHT!

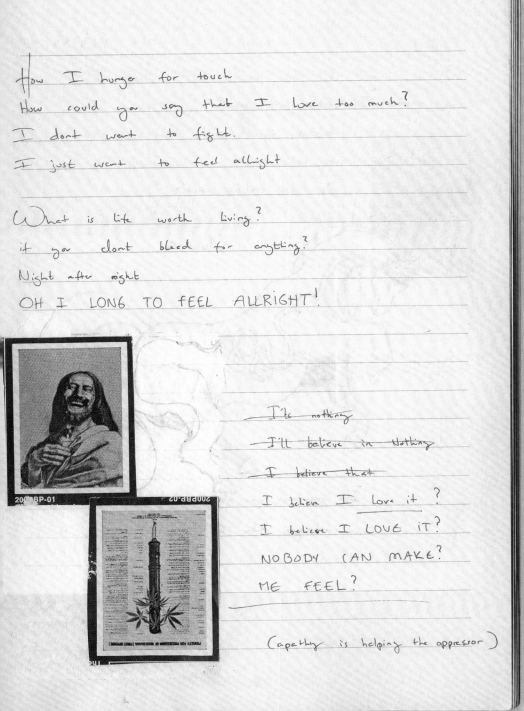

It's nothing

I'll believe in Nothing

I believe that

I believe I love it ?

I believe I LOVE iT ?

NOBODY CAN MAKE?

ME FEEL ?

(apathy is helping the oppressor)

The Essence

In another life
Home feels like home
I've mourned you now
Longer than I've known you
As the trees cry their leaves
Vulnerable
Just like me

Maybe, maybe it will be alright?
We all hurt sometimes
Maybe, maybe it will be alright?
We are running through the waves of time
And the truth can lie, in the arms of a fight
And I try, and I try
But it hurts so much
To be in touch
So, I'd rather not

We make amends with the roads we cross
Like rivers flow
To be near your ground

Maybe, maybe it will be alright?
We all hurt sometimes
Maybe, maybe it will be alright?
We are running through the waves of time
And the truth can lie, in the arms of a fight
And I try, and I try
But it hurts so much
To be in touch
With the essence of us

It hurts so much
To be in touch
With the essence of us
With the essence of us
It hurts so much
To be in touch
So, I'd rather not

"It hurts so much
to be in touch

So I'd rather not."

THE ESSENCE

In another life... Home feels like Home
I've mourned you now .... longer than I've known you
As the trees ... cry their leaves
~~The~~ Vulnerable.   Just like me.

Maybe, Maybe it will be allright
we all but sometimes
Maybe, Maybe it will be allright
We are running through the waves of time
And the truth can lie in the arms of the night
and I try, and I try but It hurts so much.
                              to be in touch.
                              So I'd rather not.

We make amends.
with the roads we cross.
Like rivers flow.....   to be near your ground.

It hurts so much. to be in touch.
With the essence of us. with the essence of us.
It hurts so much
to be in touch.   so I'd rather not.

I see more and more
the journey I've been on myself
in this album.
I've had so much pain to make sense of.
this album might be more personal
than I am comfortebe with.
But then again.
I always tell the world to open up.
so why cant I?

THE DOG THAT
BIT ITSELF.

I feel like a dog
biting its own tail.
yes. not chasing. biting.
Which is odd.
Cause I'm such a cat person.
May all cats live forever.

ALBUM TRACK LIST #1

I think I have too much to say. 14 tracks is not enough.

1. The echo of my shadow
2. Some type of skin
3. Your blood
4. the Conflict of the mind   Needs to flow.
5.
6. the essence   ?
7.   soulsearcher?
8. Dreams   forget your body?
9. Earthly delights   feel allright?
10. The dark dresses lightly   A soul with no king?
11.   Bleeding black?
12.   do you feel?
13.   A word is a weapon?
14. Starvation
15. The blade
16. Invisible wounds

Needs to build. confuse. Why are
ve breaking apart? Avoiding our wounds?
the build of apathy. Hardness.

DREAMS

I've needed so much
With nothing to touch
Floating from earth

Another bridge burned
A mother concerned
"Come back to the world"

In my dreams
Everything's more quiet than here
In my dreams
Everything I feel disappears

The night became new
And out of it grew
The hymn of the pearl

Don't lie to yourself
Don't lie to the world
Don't lie to a girl

When your shadows were forgiven
I abandoned your religion
And I knew that I would never come back

So tired and so aimless
I travelled through the darkness
So my path would be impossible to track

In my dreams
Everything's more quiet than here
In my dreams
Everything I feel disappears

Learn my body and my poems
And repeat them like you own them
Like the arrow and the willow
We all bend
Let the mothers and the daughters
Climb out of the waters
Like the needle and the cockroach
We all mend

In my dreams
Everything's more quiet than here

if "peace" is continuing like we
were, with so many people suffering
...only silently....
I do not think we want peace.

We want liberation.

"IN MY DREAMS"

When your shadows were forgiven
I abandoned your religion
And I knew that
I would never come back

So tired and so aimless
I travelled through the darkness
So my path would be

Impossible to track.

In my
dreams...

Everything's more
quiet than here

Learn my body
and my poems
and repeat them
like you own them

like the arrow, and the willow
we all bend

Let the mother
and the daughters
Climb out of the water

like the needle
and the cockroach

we all mend

IN MY DREAMS

As I've needed so much
with nothing to touch...
floating from earth

(8) Song number 8. I promised my mother.

Another bridge burned
A mother concerned
"Come back to the world"

In my dreams ... everything's more quiet than here
In my dreams ... everything I feel disappears

The ~~singlob~~ right became new
        and out of it grew
        the hymn of the ~~pearld~~ pearl

Don't lie to yourself
don't lie to the world
dont lie to a girl

In my dreams ... everythings more quiet tha here
In my dreams... everything I feel... disappears

The female intellect. Women's intellect is manifested as perfect control, presence of mind, and utilization of all advantages. They bequeath it as their fundamental character to their children, and the father furnishes the darker background of will. His influence determines the rhythm and harmony, so to speak, to which the new life is to be played out; but its melody comes from the woman.

To say it for those who know how to explain a thing: women have the intelligence, men the heart and passion.

"We're good people....
  And we both deserve

            peace"

drawing   by : eeurckaa

me.

if I had

long hair.

HISTORY of THE HEART

in the Seventeenth century
the elite scottish couples
adressed eachother with
terms of endearment.

expressions such as "sweetheart"
and "My dearest heart"
grew common amongst men
and women.
in secrecy most likely
between men and men, and
woman to woman.

the beloved was not an
arm. or a kidney, or
a rib — but a heart.

the heart did not only
serve expressions of love
but also as a barometer
of morality.
to be "blackhearted"
or to be "kindhearted".

the heart could, and did —
stand for the whole person.
to "learn by heart."

their desires.

their thoughts.

their life immortal.

A poem:

"I dont love you just from the bottom of
my heart, I love you from the top and middle too"

— by, Virgil (a roman poet) (between 29 and 19 BC):-

this year I have ~~this~~ truly learnt
How dark life can become
How lonely you can find
yourself within the cambers of
your own heart
                    It is such a physichal ache
I've hurt myself a lot.
and each time I do, I only seem
to spiral further in and down into that
darkness. and in the ache.
And the next morning when I awake
I find myself at the bottom, looking up
                    feeling like I might never
                    come up again.

I feel guilty for hurting myself
cause right now I need so much love.
I dont want to be - just a wound.
I want to be so much more.

what happened to me was painful.
But it was also very beautiful.

Then came the big perspective.
then came the wish of feeling better.
Then came the thoughts of giving up
Just escaping my own self
allowing the dark to
be something i dance with.
then came the desperate need
for something truthful and pure.

Starvation.

then the rage.
and then finally the realization
I am wounded.
And what is wounded needs to mend
What happened to the heart?

What happened to the heart?

EARTHLY DELIGHTS

First you made for me a river
So I would have water
Made for me a garden
So I would have earth

But I'm so lonely
So lonely
When everything dies
Can you stay with me?

Could you give to me desire
So I would have fire
Fill my lungs with air
I'll be a perfect lover

But I'm so lonely
So lonely
If everything dies
Why can't you love me?

And when time at last consumes me
Broken and unholy
Let my body wander far away from here
You make for me a portal
Eyes warmed up with sorrow
You always envied mortals
'Cause we can leave

There is no god in here without me, my dear
When everything dies
Will you be lonely?
So lonely
So lonely...

EARTHLY DELIGHTS

A story about a god
who loved a woman so much
He made her a new planet

then he put her there
all by herself
Away from all earthly temptations
away from anyone – but himself.

He made for her a river
                        so she would have water
a garden
so she would have earth
fire
so she would have desire
filled my lungs   with air
                         shall   be   the   perfect
                         lover

" But I'm so , lonely ... so lonely..."

the Wonders of life, are indeed
    delightful, but less so — experienced alone.

                        And then with time.
                        comes the inevitable.
                        Death.

"Wha' time at last, consumes me"
"let my body wander — far away from here"

"you always envied mortals....

                    cause we can leave"

                    in the end.
                    God "himself" remains alone

(God → Human)

                    "there is no god
                        in her without me
                            my dear."

                            REAL LYRICS —)

"If I was a pigeon, would I shit on everyone?"
(pigeon??)

I do not know What this means
it may be unsettling
But its also
so Beautic

I have this feeling
they might never manage to
fly. Each head pulling
the swan in different direction

You look so pretty
When you cry
come back here
come alive.

Bring your past
bring your ghosts...

Bring your pain,
and I'll bring mine.

We'll be fine.
But first, we must struggle

When the "Politics" of
        the World splits the people

"from empathy to Apathy
            the biggest enemy of progress"

"Rage vs. silence"

We are scaring eachother
away from speaking up, when the
empathy we have in us
tells us that what we
see is wrong.

When people are only told
"the heart vs. the mind"   to "educate themselves" when
                            trying to empathically engage
                            in the world
                            that empathy will die.
                            And we will remain afraid
                            of speaking up. when somet
                            is wrong.

"peace vs. liberation"

people who want you to stay quiet
may be bothered by you simply
engaging in matters they want
to be left alone.

"Peace" for them, may be your
silence.
But then again, your <u>silence</u> may
contribute to the suffering of so many
others.

I understand why people are confused.
But I don't think we should
let our minds scare us away
from feeling the way we do, about
the matters of the <u>heart.</u>

I refuse to believe people are <u>evil.</u>
I think people are scared. and confused.
which makes us... Apathic.

are we more concerned by feeling <u>better</u>
than cohotic?
               than to achieve <u>actual</u> progress??????

WHEN THE DARK DRESSES LIGHTLY

As I pour out my story
Drink me up
There is wine in every word
(Here's to us now, my dear
We're being strong now)

And the dark dresses lightly
Razor sharp
As it cuts right through my soul
(Here's to us now, my dear
It took too long)

Guess I shouldn't have kept the knife in my heart for so long
Guess I shouldn't have held back when I needed you to know
Guess I shouldn't have kept the knife in my heart for so long
Guess I shouldn't have held back when I needed you to know

Ooo I just want to cry
With you tonight
It's perfectly fine
To grieve the hurt that's gonna die

Let us dance to our sorrow
Make amends
There's so much you still don't know
(Here's to us now, my dear
We're going deep now)

All this fear
It's contagious
Now we're here
Let our glasses overflow
(Here's to us now, my dear
It took too long)

Guess I shouldn't have kept the knife in my heart for so long
Guess I shouldn't have held back when I needed you to know
Guess I shouldn't have kept the knife in my heart for so long
Guess I shouldn't have held back when I needed you to know

Ooo I just want to cry
With you tonight
It's perfectly fine
To grieve the hurt that's gonna die

Oh, oh, oh
Can you feel it?
Mmmhhh yeah
Let me feel it
Louder
Louder!
Louder!!
Louder!!!

To the river
To the water
Where the floodgates
Are wide open
And the tower
Has fallen onto you
Let me feel it darling
(Darling, darling)
Let me feel it darling

Oh yeah!!

(TENSION!!)

As I pour out my story
dink me up.... there is wine in every word.

"HERE'S TO US NOW,
MY DEAR.   ⌐— CHOIR!?!
WE'RE BEING STRONG NOW"

And the dark ... dresses lightly
Razor sharp ... as it cuts right through my soul

"HERE'S TO US NOW
MY DEAR.
IT TOOK TOO LONG"

Guess I shouldn't have kept the knife
in my heart for so long
Guess I shouldn't have held back
When I needed you to know ↰ *100000w

"the DARK DRESSES LIGHTLY"

(some kind of sensual intro??)

"oooo" oh I just want to cry!
   ↳ With you tonight!
   ↳ Oh, I'ts perfectly fine
         To grieve the HURT that's gonna die

Let us dance, tour Sorrow....
...Make amends... There's so much you still dont know

"HERE'S TO US NOW,
my DEAR.
WE'RE GOING DEEP NOW"

All this fear, its contagious
Now WE'RE HERE
LET OUR GLASSES OVERFLOW!!

"HERE'S TO US NOW
my DEAR
IT TOOK TOO LONG"

mmhh yeah......

....let me feel
it .....

I was just in Germany
With my two Beloved friends Nico and Mich[ael]

We cried. We had the whole world in our
hearts. We drank so much wine.
and I danced so much in th studio
that my feet still HURT.

I'ts delicious to be so alive.

"THe dark dresses lightly"

might be. one of my favorite songs I've ever
Written. Though I know, or at least assume
I't going to take a while for the world
to understand.

But that is ok.
It is my child. and i Love it. with all
my being. I am so Happy.

LAST MINUTE LYRIC!!

NEED TO END!! ORGASMIC.

"oh yeah, oh YEAH!
LOUDER!!!
Let me feel it!!

"To the rivers
to the waters
Where the floodgates are wide open

And the Tower, has fallen ontoo you"

Confrontation
is orgasmic
this song needs
to feel just like it.

A Soul With No King

I know you know me
And you always will
Like a man with no wisdom
And a soul with no king

I know you fear me
Your heart unfulfilled
Like a world with no mother
And a home never built

But if this is what you want
Why speak of right and wrong
You still go in for the kill

You speak of the devil
Like he's not your friend
When the world starts to burn
Give your water to him

Call my name
Call my name

Nothing will ever change
No guilt
No shame
Call out my name
When you need me again
Nothing will ever change
No guilt
No shame
Call out my name
When you need me again

If you know who I am
Why won't you call my name?
If you know who I am
Why won't you call my name?
You know who I am
Why won't you call my name?
You know who I am
Why won't you call my name?

"A SOUL WITH NO KING"

I know you know me...
and you always will....
like a man, with no wisdom
and a soul with no king..

I know you fear me...
Your heart unfulfilled
like a world with no mother
And a home never built

But if this
is what you want, why....
Speak of right and wrong
you
still...
so in for the kill

(SCREAM. WITH THE RAGE OF MOTHER EARTH)

you speak of the devil
Like he's not your friend
When the world starts to burn
give your water to him

(whisper --- "call my name") ⤷ who am I?

Nothing will ever change
No guilt
No shame
Call out my name...
...When you need me again.

...if you know who I am..
why wont you call my name?

(Written some day in
September 2023)

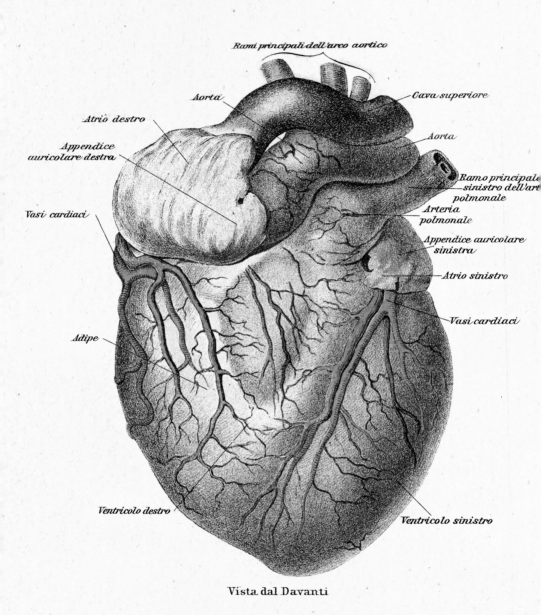

Rami principali dell'arco aortico

Aorta

Atrio destro

Appendice
auricolare destra

Vasi cardiaci

Adipe

Ventricolo destro

Cava superiore

Aorta

Ramo principale
sinistro dell'art.
polmonale

Arteria
polmonale

Appendice auricolare
sinistra

Atrio sinistro

Vasi cardiaci

Ventricolo sinistro

Vista dal Davanti

IL CUORE

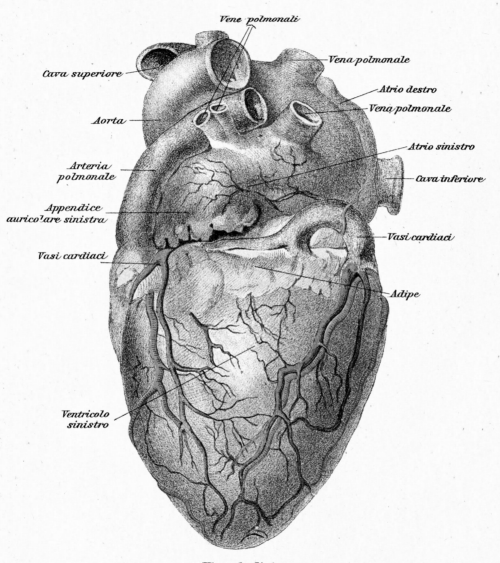

Vene polmonali

Cava superiore

Vena polmonale

Atrio destro

Vena polmonale

Aorta

Atrio sinistro

Arteria
polmonale

Cava inferiore

Appendice
auricolare sinistra

Vasi cardiaci

Vasi cardiaci

Adipe

Ventricolo
sinistro

Vista da Sinistra

L' UOMO.

"Some of the saddest
people I know...

...are Happy...
all the time.

-A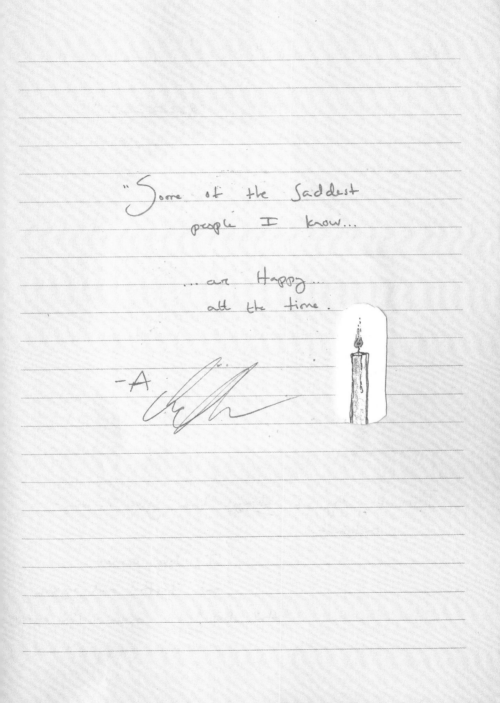

"BZZZZZZST"

This is why I always have glue in my
backpack.

I love armour.
and teeth. and organs.
this does not mean I'm cra

My Name

My name
Was hidden somewhere
In the back of my brain
I didn't know before my head was drained
And all I could hear was that name

I erase
The mission I had before I was reversed
Long before I was a part of earth
I was a part of your world
I was a part of your world
I was a part of your world

The parade
An innocent way to teach a dying cell
You eventually will be eaten by yourself
Nobody asks for help

Far away
Somebody was given just another year
Another departure in our atmosphere
Will you forget I was here?
Will you forget I was here?
Will you forget I was here?
Will you forget I was here?

Will you forget I was here?
Will you forget I was here?

"GIVE UP"
Don't give up
Your people care
I need you here

MY NAME

my name
was hidden somewhere, in the back of my brain
I didn't know, before my head was drained

and all I could hear
was that name

I erase
the mission I had before I was reversed
long before I was a part, of earth

I was a part of your world

The parade
an innocent way to teach a dying cell
you eventually will be eaten by yourself

Nobody's asking for help

far away
Somebody was given just another year
another departure in our atmosphere

will you forget I was here?
Will you forget I was here?
Will you forget I was here?

(HYMN) ⭐

"GIVE UP"
dont give up
"GIVE UP"
dont give up

I need you here

(I THINK I NEED A DISCO SONG)

(TO WRITE ONE)

(BUT DON'T TELL ANYONE)

MADE BY A GENIOUS

WARRIOR SOMEWHERE

IN A GALAXY FAR FAR AWAY.....

Do You Feel?

Never give up this feeling
Never give up on love
You can give up on me
But never give up on love

In our bodies and in our bones
We both sing in deeper tones
In the fire, we both run to hide
And you let the sun call my name
And we dance in her flames
So warm
I feel love, love, love

Do you feel love?
You got me burning
But I can't stop
It feels like I need it

But I can't stop
It feels like I need it

Never give up this feeling
Never give up on love
You can give up on me
But never give up on love
Never give up this feeling
Never give up on love
You can give up on me
But never give up on love

Do you feel love?
You got me burning
But I can't stop
It feels like I need it

(What do you believe in?)
I believe in bleeding, for love
(What do you believe in?)
I believe in bleeding, for love

Do you feel love?
You got me burning
But I can't stop
It feels like I need it

You can give up on me
But never give up on love

DO YOU FEEL?

      NEVER GIVE UP THIS FEELING

      NEVER GIVE UP ON LOVE

      YOU CAN GIVE UP ON ME

      BUT NEVER GIVE UP ON LOVE

In our bodies and in our bones
we both speak in deeper tones
into the fire
we'll both run, to hide...

So we let the sun call our names
and we'd dance in her flames

So warm...
I feel love.

Do YOU FEEL LOVE?

YOU, YOU GOT ME BURNING

BUT I CAN'T STOP

IT FEELS LIKE I NEED IT

FREEDOM

200RRR-05

Laughing Jesus

What do we choose to see??

This is one of the only times
In my life
where I've written an album
whilst allowing the world in.

I haven't escaped somewhere, or secluded myself.
I've carried it all with me.
it has felt completely right
and totally un-avoidable.
to the children of
Palestine. of Ghana.   even though the world
you've been with   manages to disagree on so
during this whole process.   much   ?!
                                When so many unneccessary
Such bloodshed.   ~~lives are~~ Deaths are taking
Such trauma.   place.
inflicted on real people.   it seems like we are not
Whatever we call it   on the right path. at all.
I cannot help   This is not the kind of
but to view it   world we deserve.
as such a cruel   indeed. What happened to the heart.
an Inhumane act.
devastating.

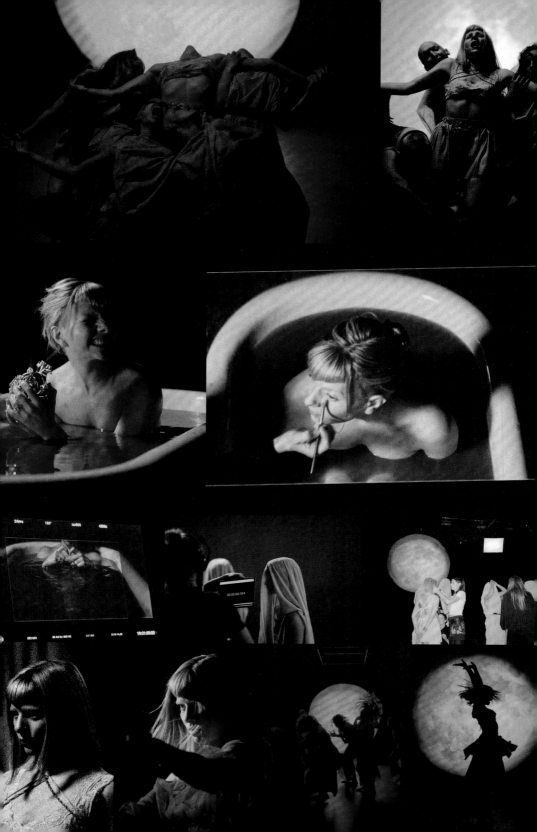

STARVATION

I miss the touch of human hands on my skin
Miss the rush of beauty coming from within
Do I need to be torn?
Just to see who will care?
I sleep on the floor
Dreaming my life away

Why do we have to die for us to see the light?
And we hunger for love
Why do we touch the knife when we long to feel alive?
And we hunger for love
And my soul is starving

Come on over, take a bite of the last apple here on Earth
Will the virtual mind become stronger than mine?
And when my ego dies
Will I stay here forever?
When the Webb crashes down
Will my life be better?

Why do we have to die for us to see the light?
And we hunger for love
And my soul is starving
Why do we touch the knife when we long to feel alive?
And we hunger for love
And my soul is starving

Break me, break me
Chasing the enemy
Got a deal with the devil but
I got the stamina
Higher than anything
I've ever seen or been
Right now everything
Everything's empty
Starving, craving
Chasing the remedy
I got used to the torture
But no one deserves to be alone
They break me
Chasing the enemy
And my soul is hurting
But I got the stamina!!

(Why do we have to die for us to see the light?)
(We are decorated bones and my soul is starving)

(MY SOUL)
(MY SOUL)
(MY SOUL IS STARVING)
(I'M DYING)

MAKE ME BREAK ME

CHASING THE ENEMY

GOT A DEAL WITH THE DEVIL BUT

I GOT THE STAMINA!!!!

HIGHER THAN ANYTHING, IVE EVER SEEN OR BEEN

BUT RIGHT NOW

EVERYTHING.

EVERYTHINGS EMPTY!!!!

STARVING, CRAVING

CHASING THE REMEDY

I/WE?? GOT USED TO THE TORTURE

BUT NO ONE DESERVES TO BE ALONE

(REPETITIO

BREAK ME

CHASING THE ENEMY

AND MY SOUL IS HURTING

BUT I GOT THE STAMINA!!!

(Why do we have

for us to see th

(We are decorate

Bones

And our soul is s

→ AI TAKES OVER THE SO

GOD HELP US ALL!!!!

(1. OCTIVE DOWN) UNLEASH

STARVATION

I miss the touch of human hands on my skin
miss the rush of _beauty_ coming from within

①o I need to be torn?
   Just to see who will care?
I sleep on the floor
   Dreaming my life away

REF PART???

Come on over take a bite
of the last apple her on Earth
Will the virtual mind
   Become stronger than mine?

Why do we have to die?
   for us' to see the light?
   While we hunger for love?

Why do are touch the life
   When we long to feel alive
and When we hunger for love
   And my our soul is starving

And when my EGO dies
will i stay her foreve?
When th WEBB creates down
Will my life be better?

MY SOUL IS STARVING!!

START W. CLOSEUP. (20s.) BEFORE
BEAT KICKS IN.

THE DEEP.   CHOREOGRAPHY
THE ACHING HUNGER.   WILL SHOW.

                            (CALL LIV
                              LOCKWOOD)

IS ROOM
DARK OR

RED FLOOR?
RED FABRIC?

MOVING UNDER IT LIKE
WATER OR A FEATUS.
SLOW ZOOM OUT.

"WALL
OF HANDS"

RED ON
RED.
WHAT ARE
THEY
REACHING FOR?
(BLUE)

                    CLOSEUP OF HAND
                    BEATING CHEST.

                                    CLOSE

STATIC CHOREOGRAPHY
PLANTED FEET → W. RHYTM
START AT BASS RHYTM   HIT CHEST.

RED / BLUE PAINTED FEET

IN THE RHY
THE DRUM
ANGRY.

            TOWA

                    FILMED
                    SIDEWAYS

CRAWLING AFTER APPLE
2ND VERSE BEGINNING

MORE WILD CHOREOGRAPHY

1ST. DROP
DR.?   EVERYONE DANCES
              BUT M?

                    ZOOM IN
                    OR OUT

                            END

BLUE APPLE & BLUE S
HAND?
IS THE "HUNGER" BLUE
WHEN IS IT TAKING

SOUND RIGHT AT THE
SPECIAL MOVEMEN

4 v. LIPSYNC AND WITHOUT

ALL FOR END?

EVERYONE MOVES SLOW MOTION
STAND STILL.

LIGHT SOURCE
ABOVE

"I GOT THE STAMINA"

→ A MOMENT OF STILLNESS?

THEN. LET. GO.

TURN INTO HEAVY METAL
CORE.

A RITUAL?
HUMAN CONNECTION?
SACRIFIZE ot THE WOMAN?

ALL SLOW MOTION
TOWARDS END?

FEET. ALL BLUE? MOVING FASTER

ACHING
FOR
CONNECTION
WITH
EARTH
HOOF???
WTF??

"RELIGIOUS HANDS" ACHING FOR SPIRITUALITY.

(I SWEAR I KNOW HOW HANDS LOOK LIKE)

The Blade

Fall into my arms
Like you trust me
I'll keep my bloodstained hands
Off your body

Innocent like a child
Yet she sleeps with a knife right under her pillow
And the claws won't be near anymore
Paralysed in denial ever-changing
Will she be the same?
See your shame, on the wall, on the cross
In the night, nobody remembers
When she cried scarlet skies on the floor
A million doors, corridors ever-changing
I still feel the rage

Watch out, watch what you say
Your truth becomes your grave
A sword can cut both ways
But I got sharp blades
Feel the rage!

Vertigo, all she knows
When the world drags her soul deep into the shadow
Like a chain it chokes my throat when she cries
I hold her near
Hurting world, overwhelming
I still feel her pain

Watch out, watch what you say
Your truth becomes your grave
A sword can cut both ways
But I got sharp blades
Feel the rage!

Soft hearts need protection, need protection
Soft hearts need protection, need protection

Feel the rage!
Rage, I feel rage
I feel rage
I feel rage!

Soft hearts need protection, need protection
Soft hearts need protection, need protection

THE BLADE

fall into my arms
like you trust me
(But) keep my bloodstained hands
off your body

innocent like a child
yet she sleeps with a knife right under her pillow
and the claws won't be near anymore

paralyzed in denial
everchanging.... will she be the same?

See your shame on the wall
on the cross, in the night nobody remembers
When she cried scarlett skies on the floor (B

~~paralyzed~~ a million doors → corridoors
everchanging
I STILL FEEL THE RAGE (HER RAGE??)

FEEL THE RAGE!!!

WATCH OUT, WATCH WHAT
U SAY. YOUR TRUTH BECOMES
YOUR GRAVE!!!
A SWORD CAN CUT
BOTH WAYS. BUT I GOT
SHARP BLADES.

Vertigo, all she knows
as the world drags her soul
deep into the shadows
Like a chain
it chokes my throat when she cries

I hold he near
a hurting world
overwhelming
I STILL FEEL HER PAIN

(enter prodigy domain)

"Soft hearts, need protection" x2
→ x2/x4

Where the sea and heaven touches hands
I saw
        a boy go in, and leave – a man.

    I don't believe I understand
What happened to him.

My Body
Is Not Mine

I can remember the first time I felt my mind
Turning into a beast of an evil kind
If there's a demon in the line of my aim
I won't be calling its name

I would stare at the back of my hand for days
Reading the wisdom written out for me in my veins
If there's a demon in the eye of my soul
I won't be letting you know

But the light kicks in when I know it's time
I've built my walls so it's safe to hide
And the people I love I've left behind
They see too much when they look in my eyes
Feel no pain and I never cry
I bleed no blood, I will never die
My body's not mine, body's not mine
Body's not mine, I need no body
My body isn't mine

And the past feels like another life
When the story they somehow all survived
Repeats itself so many times
Written cold in blood, heavy as a bible
Feel no pain and I never cry
I bleed no blood, and I never die
My body's not mine, body's not mine
Body's not mine, I need no body

"When you need my heart"
You cry
"You need my body, body"

CEASEFIRE NOW

(91) TOM ROWLANDS!!! GET THAT CHEMICHAL BROTHERS
JUICE ON THIS BABY!!!!

and the past feels like another life
when the story they somehow all survived
repeats itself so many times
written cold in blood
heavy as a bible

"feel no pain — and never cry"
"bleed no blood — and never die"
my body's not mine
my body's not mine

I need no body

                                    "When you need my hea
                                    you cry
                                    "You need my body"
"MY BODY IS NOT MINE"   X 2 / X

                                    "Is this all you got?"

thank you M x

MY BODY IS NOT MINE

(from the point
of the predator?)
or what makes
you different
from the
predator?

I can remember the first I felt my mind
turning into a beast of an Evil kind
if there's a demon in the light of my aim
I wont be calling its name...

I would stare at the back of my hand for days
reading the wisdom written out for me in my veins
if there's a demon in the eye of my soul
(I won't bE letting you know)

But the light kicks in
when I know its time
I've built my walls, so it's safe to hide
and the people I love
I've left behind
they see too much when they look in my eyes

feel no pain - never ~~die~~ cry
bleed no blood - never die
My body's not mine (body's not mine)
I need no body

OK. SO... TRACKLIST?

What Happened To the ~~Heart~~ ?

1. Echo Of my Shadow
2. Be allright
3. ~~Conflict of The Mind~~ Your Blood
4. ~~Some Type of Skin~~ Conflict Of the Mind
5. Some type of Skin
6. Essence
7. Earthly delights
8. The dark dresses Lightly
9. A Soul with No King
10. Dreams
11. My name
12. Do you feel?
13. Starvation
14. The Black
15. My body is not mine.
16. ?

→ Invisible Wounds?

INVISIBLE WOUNDS

I squeeze into a small hole
Through the eyes of needles
To stitch you up again
Even though I know so well
I can't fix anything
I look for blood to shed
Mistaking every vein for thread
Spreading out too thin
As I'm lying in my bed, barely existing

And I need you
And I need you
To understand
To understand

Sometimes I see light
And I fear it's only fantasy
Oh, wouldn't it be tragic
If there is no light in me?
Not any magic

And I need you
To forgive me
If you can
If you can

I know the best I can
Isn't always good enough
It hurts to know I hurt you
Like I know it hurts for you
To know you've hurt me
And now my blood is yours
And life is slowly losing touch
How do we learn to tend to
These invisible wounds our homes gave us?

I can't heal you
And you can't heal me
Even if we wanted to
And how I wanted to
And I need you
To stop needing me
Like I've needed you
We both need to
Tend to the invisible wounds

Invisible Wounds

I squeeze into a small hole
through the eyes of needles
to stich you up again
even though I know so well
I can't fix anything....

I look for blood to shed
mistaking every vein for thread
spreading out too thin...
as I'm lying in my bed
barely existing

And I need you.... And I need you..... To Understand.

Sometimes I see light
and I fear it's only fantasy
Oh, Wouldn't it be tragic
if there is no light in me
not any magic

And I need you.
To forgive me.
if you can.

I can't heal you
~~And~~ you can't heal me
even if we wanted to
and how we've wanted to

. . . . . .

I know the best I can
~~teln~~ Isn't always good enough
It hurt to know I <u>hurt</u> you
like I know it hurts for you
to know you <u>hurt</u> me.

And now my blood is yours
and life is slowly loosing touch
How do we learn to tend to?
. . . these invisible wounds our <u>homes</u> gave us?

and I need you.
to stop needing me.   How
like I've needed you.   (and oh, I've needed you)
we both need to
tend to the Invisible wounds

It was the kind of truth
that only existed in
                my mind
And as I spoke it out
Loud

It became a truth
for the
Whole World

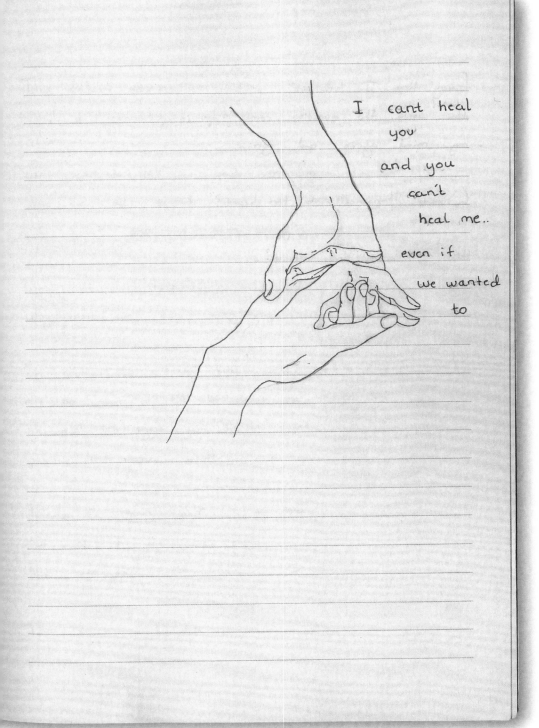

I cant heal
you
and you
can't
heal me..
even if
we wanted
to

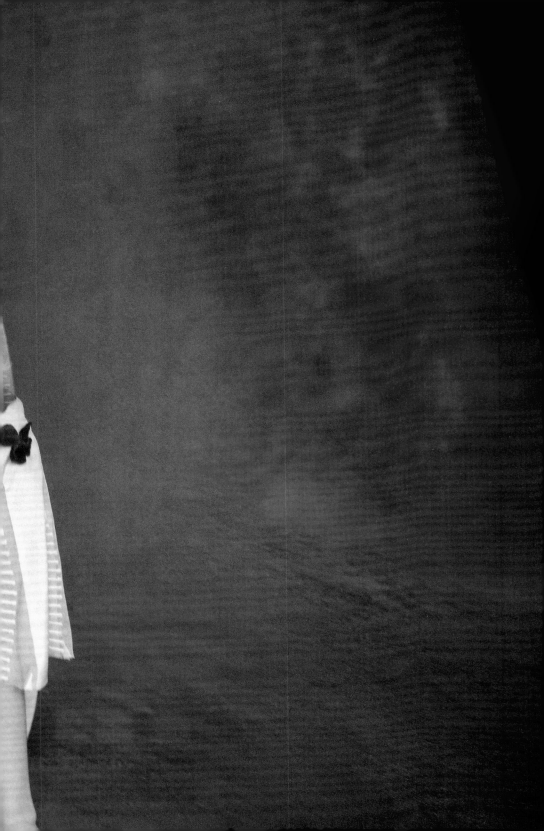

Every time I look at
the world. this question comes up in
my mind again and again.

"What Happened to the heart?"

How did we loose touch?

This Album Process is reaching its end
What an exhausting adventure.

I Just went to NY, to spend some time at the UN
where we all talked about our beloved dying Earth
and what stops us from changing our ways

Why cant we coexist?
why must we devour everything.

It seems, for a long time we've had to
rely on music and art to deliver the messages to
the people. We must join hands with
politics. and with science.

Because the truth needs to be told
but not to our minds only.
Now more than ever

The heart.

Have you ever met
Someone just like

TRIGGER ME

Everything's rising up
entangled in violence
So many defenceless
who suffer in silence

We know we feel
something is lost in
the riot
When truth is a liar
death has no triumph

And the feeling rises
wisdom's quiet
I feel frightened!!!
MOTHER!!
I choose living over dying

Who will be my saviour?

Thank you Chris for being such
a great friend
for all the fun we've had
(your a good Earthling.
→ And for yet
again
reminding me
that
"Heavy metal rules"

Thank you Ja[...]
for alway keepi[...]
on time. for be[...]
a new light.
for your help.
for everything.

Thank you Vetle ♥

Thank you to Matia Tellez
this chapter starts and ends
with song I recorded with
you. Thank you for understanding
the important of pouring
the spiritual message into
every sound. I know we will make
a lot of magic.

Thank you Nico and Michelle
when the three of us gather in a room
the world makes sense.
And what doesn't make sense yet — we pour into music.
I love you both so much.
And I appreciate you both so much.
as humans. as musicians. your very souls.

Thanks to Benedict and kayla for Spending New year eve
with me.

for being there for me
In my darkness,
Thank you ~~the~~ Magnus.
again. for being there for me.
My best friend.
Only three of our songs
are in this chapter.
But you're more a part
of "everything", than you know.
You've touched both my
heart and my mind in this life
and for that I am forever grateful.

Thank you Tom Rowlands
for picking up the phone
when I called.
When I told you to
"Vomit" on my song
you knew exactly what to do.

Thank you Sam.
Working with you is a delight.
And I am so happy to also call you a friend.

Thank you Frederik.
for being my friend.
a beam of sunshine on tour,
you lift us all.
Our child "A soul w. no king"
is my favourite piece of music. ever.

Thank you Mitch
for your touch.
having you mix
this chapter has
been a dream x.

Thank you to my dads
Lykke and Margo or
for showing me your
darkness and your light.
you inspire me more than
you know. I love you
both more than you know.

Thank you to all my lovers.
for your touch.

and for letting me be free.
I know it is not easy
to let go
of Something you love.

We held on to eachother
and then
we let go.

Thank you for loving me
and allowing free to love you.

To love, is the greatest
honor on earth.

                                    —A

Thank you to My sisters.
this all exists because of you

Miranda, may you find your light.

Viktoria, may you exist for yourself,
as much as you exist for others

And may I outlive you both.
So you never have to attend my funeral

This I promise. I will do my very best.

Listen to the plead, have more empathy.

give back the stolen land.

Apologize to the earth.

STOP the killings of innocent people.

open up your hearts.

Be better to yourself.

to life itself.

All life.

07.06.2024   What Happened To

                                      The heart?

A.R.J.S.BL.A.C.S.CC.L6.A.(M)K.NJ.C.V.N.S.A.A.I.Li
       ↑
       C

A.J.R.SBIBJA.A

C.C.S.CC.(L6).A.M.NJ.C.CS

V.N.SL.A.A.I.HH.

B.L.E.H+E.LK.

S.CWTB.S.L.V.E.VT.H.

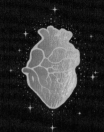

"We are the seed, the root, the forest, the rivers,
the woods, the animals, the cosmos."

Taken from *We are the Earth*
co-written by Sônia Guajajara and Célia Xakriabá

Book design by Dominic Brookman
Cover illustration by Tessa Rose Jackson
Photography by Wanda Martin © Decca

Human, All Too Human
by Friedrich Nietzsche
originally published in 1878

© 2024 by Faber Music Ltd & Decca Records
(a division of Universal Music Operations Limited)
First published in 2024 by Faber Music and
4wordhouse, on behalf of Decca Records
Faber Music
Brownlow Yard
12 Roger Street
London WC1N 2JU

4wordhouse and Decca Records are divisions of
Universal Music Operations Limited
4 Pancras Square
London N1C 4AG
fourwordhouse.com
decca.com

All lyrics reproduced by permission of Budde Music

Printed and bound in Turkey by Imago
All rights reserved.

ISBN 1: 0-571-54325-1
EAN 13: 978-0-571-54325-0

To buy Faber Music publications or to find
out about the full range of titles available
please contact your local retailer or
Faber Music sales enquiries:

Faber Music Limited, Burnt Mill, Elizabeth Way,
Harlow, CM20 2HX, England
Tel: +44 (0) 1279 82 89 82
fabermusic.com